MW00964793

BIG SPORTS BRANDS

ESPN

Top Sports News Channel

by Kristian R. Dyer

SportsZone

An Imprint of Abdo Publishing
abdobooks.com

abdobooks.com

Published by Abdo Publishing, a division of ABDO, PO Box 398166, Minneapolis, Minnesota 55439. Copyright © 2024 by Abdo Consulting Group, Inc. International copyrights reserved in all countries. No part of this book may be reproduced in any form without written permission from the publisher. SportsZone™ is a trademark and logo of Abdo Publishing.

Printed in the United States of America, North Mankato, Minnesota.
052023
092023

THIS BOOK CONTAINS
RECYCLED MATERIALS

Cover Photo: Mitchell Leff/Getty Images Sport/Getty Images
Interior Photos: Stephen Maturen/Getty Images Sport/Getty Images, 4–5; Mike Zarrilli/ Getty Images Sport/Getty Images, 6; Nick Potts/PA Images/Alamy, 7; Peter G. Aiken/Getty Images Sport/Getty Images, 9; Bruce Bennett Studios/Getty Images, 10–11; The Ring Magazine/Getty Images, 12; Robert W Stowell Jr/Archive Photos/Getty Images, 14, 17; K. Mazur/WireImage for ESPN/Getty Images, 16; Jessica Hill/AP Images, 18–19; Kevin Winter/ Getty Images Entertainment/Getty Images, 21; Kelly Sullivan/Getty Images for Eat. Learn. Play./Getty Images Entertainment/Getty Images, 22; Jamie McCarthy/Getty Images for Paley Center for Media/Getty Images Entertainment/Getty Images, 23; Pavlo Gonchar/ SOPA Images/LightRocket/Getty Images, 25; Rob Loud/Getty Images for Tribeca Film Festival/Getty Images Entertainment/Getty Images, 26; Austin McAfee/Cal Sport Media/ AP Images, 28–29; Jamie Squire/Getty Images Sport/Getty Images, 31; Kevin C. Cox/ Getty Images Sport/Getty Images, 32; Ethan Miller/Getty Images Sport/Getty Images, 35; Mike Lien/New York Times Co./Archive Photos/Getty Images, 36–37; Ethan Miller/Getty Images News/Getty Images, 39; Brian Rothmuller/Icon Sportswire/Getty Images, 41

Editors: Steph Giedd and Priscilla An
Series Designer: Joshua Olson

Library of Congress Control Number: 2022949054

Publisher's Cataloging-in-Publication Data

Names: Dyer, Kristian R., author.
Title: ESPN: top sports news channel / by Kristian R. Dyer
Other title: top sports news channel
Description: Minneapolis, Minnesota: Abdo Publishing Company, 2024 | Series: Big sports brands | Includes online resources and index.
Identifiers: ISBN 9781098290672 (lib. bdg.) | ISBN 9781098276850 (ebook)
Subjects: LCSH: ESPN, Inc.--Juvenile literature. | Sports--Equipment and supplies --Juvenile literature. | Brand name products--Juvenile literature. | Television broadcasting of sports--Juvenile literature.
Classification: DDC 658.827--dc23

TABLE OF CONTENTS

Chapter One

MONDAY NIGHT MIRACLE

Devin wakes up before school on a Monday morning. He's not concerned about his upcoming geometry test. And he hasn't given any thought to what he'll wear that day. Fantasy football is on his mind. Playing fantasy with his friends is a big way that Devin follows the National Football League (NFL). Through ESPN and its various properties, he has practically everything he needs.

Before the NFL season, Devin created a fantasy league on ESPN's website, ESPN.com. He opens up the ESPN Fantasy app on his phone to check this week's score. His team is trailing his best friend Greg's team

Fantasy football provides fans another way to engage with their favorite players, such as Justin Jefferson of the Minnesota Vikings.

by 16 points. Luckily for Devin, he has one player yet to play. Wide receiver Justin Jefferson and the Minnesota Vikings are set to play that night. Meanwhile, all of Greg's players are done for the weekend. That means a big performance by Jefferson could seal a win for Devin's team. He can't wait to watch the game on *Monday Night Football*, which is broadcast each week on ESPN.

During study hall, Devin goes to ESPN.com on his laptop. An article by an ESPN sportswriter explains how the Vikings use Jefferson in different ways. The writer projects that Jefferson's matchup against the Dallas Cowboys will earn a good number of fantasy points.

After school, Devin and Greg work out together. The TVs at the gym are playing ESPN, and *NFL Live* is on. The show is previewing the Vikings-Cowboys game.

Erin Andrews became a prominent sports broadcaster when she joined ESPN in 2004.

An ESPN camera operator shoots game action from the sideline.

An analyst shows highlights of Cowboys cornerback Trevon Diggs. Opposing wide receivers haven't caught many passes against him. It could be a rough night for Jefferson.

Devin goes over to Greg's house, and they turn on ESPN's pregame show. Once the game kicks off, Devin's nerves settle. The Vikings' offense runs through Jefferson the entire game. During the game, Diggs goes down hard, hurting his ankle. As Diggs exits the game for the day, Greg complains, "Are you serious? There goes my win." "Don't jinx it," Devin says nervously.

Despite Devin's concerns, Jefferson has a monster performance. He even scores a touchdown for the Vikings. Devin shows off the 25 points next to Jefferson in the fantasy app. "Better luck next week," he gloats.

The Worldwide Leader

ESPN long described itself as "The Worldwide Leader in Sports." Its flagship channel is broadcast in many countries. But it wasn't originally meant to be the biggest sports channel in the world. ESPN started in 1979 in Bristol, a small town in Connecticut. Cable TV was emerging as an option for people to get more channels, and ESPN's founders originally wanted their channel to cover local Connecticut sports teams. That idea expanded to a 24-hour sports news station. To fill that much time, the network began broadcasting live events. ESPN's first live broadcast was a game from the American Professional Slowpitch Softball World Series. As the network's reputation grew, it added bigger and bigger events. In addition to college sports, ESPN eventually aired games from every major American professional sport. It also broadcasts international sporting events, including soccer's World Cup games.

ESPN now provides sports fans with almost any service they could want. The main channel still broadcasts some of the biggest sporting events in the world. More than 10 million people regularly watch *Monday Night Football* on ESPN. Additional channels, such as ESPN2 and ESPNU, provide more viewing options. ESPN.com is the most visited sports website in the world, providing breaking news, sports analysis, fantasy sports platforms, and much more.

An average of 13.8 million fans watched ESPN's *Monday Night Football* each week during the 2022 season.

ESPN has also produced hundreds of sports documentaries. Its streaming service, ESPN+, has more than 24 million subscribers and original content from athletes like Peyton Manning and Tom Brady. ESPN Radio stations are available around the country. Meanwhile, mobile apps keep fans engaged on their devices. ESPN's headquarters remain in Bristol, Connecticut. And it still connects with sports fans around the world 24 hours a day.

Chapter Two

FATHER-SON START-UP

Bill Rasmussen was fired as the communications manager for the New England Whalers, a hockey team in Hartford, Connecticut, in 1978. Sports had always been his passion. He now had the freedom to pursue that passion however he wanted.

Rasmussen met Ed Eagan while he was working for the Whalers. Eagan was an insurance agent. But he always wanted to work in the television business. Shortly after he was fired, Rasmussen received a call from Eagan, and they came up with a plan for a sports program. They wanted to run a monthly cable show

Hockey star Wayne Gretzky, *right*, pretends to interview Edmonton Oilers teammate Paul Coffey using an ESPN microphone with the network's original logo in 1982.

Numerous satellite dishes can be spotted at ESPN's headquarters in Bristol, Connecticut.

focused on the Whalers and other Connecticut sports. Their conversation led to even more ideas. They eventually settled on creating an entire network that focused on Connecticut sports. Because it would be tough to fill on-air hours with just regional sports, they added some entertainment programming. That's how the channel's name was born. Rasmussen decided to call it ESP, which was short for the Entertainment and Sports Programming Network.

The idea soon expanded beyond just the state of Connecticut. Rasmussen and his son, Scott, started working on how they could broadcast the channel. They learned about satellite communications and were directed to the Radio Corporation of America (RCA). Bill and Scott learned from RCA about a transponder they had available. Using this device, they could broadcast ESP across the country for free. And it would also be cheaper for them to broadcast 24 hours a day, not for just five hours as they had originally planned. They had a new broadcasting plan. But they needed a place to put the transponder.

The Rasmussens had a site picked out in the small town of Plainville, Connecticut. But Plainville didn't allow satellite dishes. Bill found a new option in Bristol, Connecticut, instead. There was an open space of land that had earlier been a trash dump. It ended up being the perfect place for a satellite dish. Rasmussen bought the plot of land for $18,000.

Finding Rights

Now that the Rasmussens had everything set up to broadcast a cable channel, they needed sports to show on the channel. Bill started ESP with his own money and some personal loans from family members. That was good enough to buy the transponder and get him a plot of land in Bristol. Buying sports rights was far more expensive, though. Rasmussen met with investors to raise money. The main investor ended up being Stuart Evey, who was the vice president of Getty Oil. Evey talked with the head of popular cable channel Home Box Office (HBO) about the possibility of investing in ESP as well. The HBO head famously told Evey, "There's no way anybody will watch sports 24 hours a day."

ESP's main attraction at the time was college sports. Rights to broadcast them were much cheaper to buy than those for professional leagues. College sports were also not broadcast regularly in the late 1970s, despite being popular. Rasmussen met with the National Collegiate Athletic Association (NCAA) and struck a deal. The main prize was broadcasting rights to college basketball. The NCAA told ESP that if it wanted to show these games, it also had to buy the rights to broadcast 17 less popular sports as well. That was perfect for Rasmussen. He had to fill 8,760 hours of live television a year.

ESPN commentator Dick Vitale shoots some hoops before a University of Connecticut game in 1990.

With those added sports, Evey was convinced he could fill the time. In March 1979, he officially signed a contract to invest in ESP. The timing worked out well. The NCAA Division I men's basketball tournament was underway. Two weeks after the contract was signed, the national championship game was played. It featured the two biggest young stars in basketball. Indiana State was led by Larry Bird. The opposing Michigan State team featured star guard Earvin "Magic" Johnson. Over the next 12 years, the two would go on to dominate the National Basketball Association (NBA). Everyone wanted to see the game. The championship drew 35.1 million curious basketball fans when it aired on NBC. The two stars got fans excited about the sport. ESP had the rights to air college basketball starting the next season. And cable providers started receiving a lot of calls from customers asking for "that channel that has all the basketball."

What's in a Name?

ESP was signing some big sponsorship deals. But Bill Rasmussen wanted to make ESP more recognizable to advertisers. He realized all the big networks had three letters as their names: NBC, CBS, and ABC. Rasmussen decided to differentiate his by adding an *N* to the end of ESP. On July 13, 1979, the channel officially became known as ESPN.

While this was happening, Evey was taking more control

Simpler Is Better

ESPN originally stood for the Entertainment and Sports Programming Network. That was the corporation's full name until 1985. That year, the company shortened its official name to ESPN, Inc.

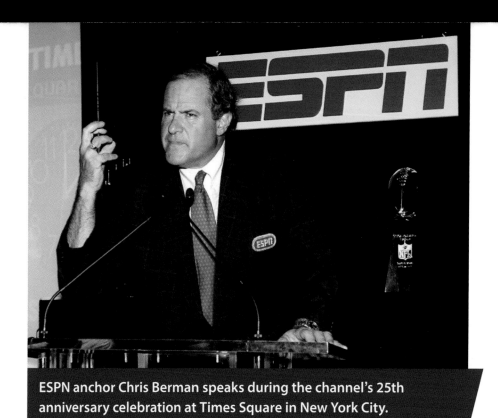

ESPN anchor Chris Berman speaks during the channel's 25th anniversary celebration at Times Square in New York City.

of the business decisions. In July 1979, he hired Chet Simmons to be the president of ESPN. Simmons had been the head of NBC Sports.

Simmons and Evey began hiring anchors and announcers for the network. Among their early hires were Bob Ley and Chris Berman. They would both go on to work for ESPN for decades.

This all led up to the launch of the network. At 7 p.m. on September 7, 1979, ESPN aired to an estimated 30,000 viewers. Lee Leonard, an anchor who left NBC Sports for ESPN, greeted the audience: "If you love sports, if you really love sports, you'll think you've died and gone to sports heaven."

ESPN commentator Robin Roberts, *right*, interviews University of Connecticut women's basketball coach Geno Auriemma before an exhibition game in 1998.

That was followed by a 30-minute broadcast of *SportsCenter* hosted by George Grande, an anchor who had come from CBS. The popular highlights show continues to be ESPN's flagship program.

ESPN's first live sporting event aired after *SportsCenter*. It was Game 1 of the American Professional Slowpitch Softball League World Series. While that wasn't as popular as the Major League Baseball (MLB) World Series, Bill and Scott Rasmussen were in awe that their idea had made it off the ground. Before the first show aired, the father and son went for a walk together and hugged each other. They didn't know at the time that what they had just launched would become the biggest sports channel in the world.

Chapter Three

MUST-SEE TV

Sports highlights are as accessible as ever. They get shared all over social media. There are a lot of apps meant for watching highlights or sharing scores from games. Before smartphones, and even before the internet, there was *SportsCenter*. It was fitting that ESPN's first broadcast was an episode of *SportsCenter*, as it would go on to be the most popular show on the network.

The early years of the show featured Chris Berman and Bob Ley, among other anchors. The focus of the show was on sports highlights. However, the

On top of sports highlights, *SportsCenter* also airs live interviews.

This is SportsCenter

The popularity of *SportsCenter* led to the show getting its own ad campaign. In 1995 commercials started airing with the show's anchors interacting with star athletes in bizarre ways. Sometimes the anchors would act like athletes. Other times the athletes would be doing normal tasks in the ESPN offices. The commercials would always end with the show's tagline of "This is *SportsCenter*" showing on the screen.

anchors describing the highlights went on to become stars themselves. Each brought a different style to how they described the action. And most of them had catchphrases that fans hooked onto.

Berman became famous for football highlights. He would yell "Whoop!" when players made shifty moves to avoid defenders. He also came up with nicknames for athletes based on pop culture references and wordplay. For example, he added "be home" in the middle of Hall of Fame baseball pitcher Bert Blyleven's name. That made it sound like "be home by 11."

Stuart Scott anchored *SportsCenter* from 1997 to 2014. He would describe athletes who performed well under pressure as being "as cool as the other side of the pillow." His go-to catchphrase was yelling "Booyah!" after an athlete made a big play.

The height of *SportsCenter* happened from 1992 to 1997 when Dan Patrick and Keith Olbermann anchored together. The duo turned the hour-long highlight show into

During his battle with terminal cancer in 2014, Stuart Scott was given the Jimmy V Award for Perseverance at that year's ESPYs.

a comedy. They regularly made jokes about the sports they were describing. They eventually nicknamed their hour of *SportsCenter* "The Big Show." Patrick and Olbermann became so popular that executives at ESPN wanted them to tone down their humor. That only led to the duo making inside jokes on the air about those executives. Olbermann left ESPN in 1997, and the partnership was over. But the duo did one last show together in 2019, as part of ESPN's 40th anniversary.

The rise of instantly available highlights on the internet led to a decrease in the popularity of *SportsCenter*. But it still airs on ESPN multiple times a day. The version that airs after the night's main sporting event is anchored by Scott Van Pelt, who has worked at ESPN since 2001. In addition to highlights, Van Pelt's show often features interviews or other segments with fellow ESPN employees.

Embrace Debate

SportsCenter carried a lot of live hours for ESPN. Its main edition aired at night to recap the day in sports, but the show aired on the channel throughout the day as well. That started to change after 2000. ESPN began to fill its daytime hours with talk shows centered on sports. The first show of that model to air on ESPN was *Pardon the Interruption* (*PTI*) in October 2001. The show featured cohosts Michael Wilbon and Tony Kornheiser, who were both writers at the *Washington Post*. The 30-minute show was designed for the cohosts to talk about the biggest topics and news stories in sports that day.

Michael Wilbon is one of the hosts of *Pardon the Interruption*.

Stephen A. Smith, *left*, and Skip Bayless, *right*, rose to fame because of their back-and-forth debates on the show *First Take*.

To stay within the 30 minutes of airtime, each topic had a time limit for how long it could be discussed. The show became very popular, with hundreds of thousands of viewers per episode.

Pardon the Interruption sparked a new era at ESPN. The channel started creating more opinion-based talk shows. A year after *PTI* debuted, ESPN created *Around the Horn*. Tony Reali, who served as the fact checker on *PTI*, became *Around the*

Horn's longtime host. Reali listens to four analysts talk about different sports topics, and he scores them. The show became a sport itself, with a winner each episode.

This led to the creation of *First Take* in 2007. *First Take* was designed to be a one-on-one debate show with a host to keep the topics on track. The show's popularity grew in 2012 when longtime analyst Skip Bayless was joined by on-air personality Stephen A. Smith. The duo would get into heated debates over their different opinions. They often disagreed with each other, which created more drama on the show.

Bayless left ESPN in 2016. Max Kellerman replaced him as Smith's debate partner. At the time, *First Take* was still airing on ESPN2, one of ESPN's partner channels. But as *SportsCenter* became less popular, ESPN began shifting its daytime schedule. *First Take* took over the main daytime slot on ESPN from 10 a.m. to noon (EST) in 2017, replacing *SportsCenter*. A year after this switch, ESPN started airing *Get Up!*, a daily morning talk show. This showed ESPN's full commitment to switching from highlight-based shows to opinion-based shows.

Let's Get Digital

While ESPN started out as a television company, it has expanded the products it offers over the years. ESPN.com launched in April 1995. The website started as a place to see

John Skipper was president of ESPN from 2012 to 2017.

breaking sports news as it happened. It evolved a few years later, once John Skipper took over control of the website.

Skipper successfully launched *ESPN The Magazine* in 1998. He then wanted the website to look like a magazine. Skipper hired a number of writers who had different backgrounds. Some came from newspapers or popular sports publications

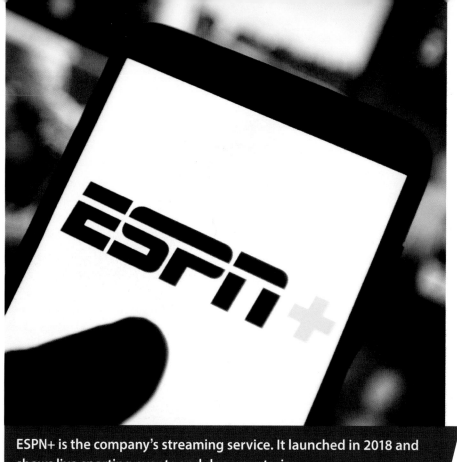

ESPN+ is the company's streaming service. It launched in 2018 and shows live sporting events and documentaries.

like *Sports Illustrated*. One of the hires, Hunter S. Thompson, had covered politics, pop culture, and sports for *Rolling Stone* magazine since the 1970s. He had also written multiple popular books, including *Fear and Loathing in Las Vegas*. Thompson was known for his unpredictable behavior and unique writing style.

Skipper also hired a Boston sports blogger named Bill Simmons. The young writer had created his own website and blog called the Boston Sports Guy. His blend of humor and sports proved popular with fans. Once ESPN brought

Simmons on board, he became a superstar in the industry. And he didn't change his writing style while he was there. While most sportswriters are trained to not have bias toward one team, Simmons still rooted for Boston in his columns.

In April 2018, the company launched its own streaming service, ESPN+. The service began as a way for ESPN to show more live sporting events. It streamed certain events that weren't shown on ESPN's other channels. For example, ESPN+ streamed MLB Spring Training games, exclusive Ultimate Fighting Championship (UFC) matches, multiple European soccer league matches, and thousands of college sporting events. ESPN also created its own original shows for the streaming service such as *The Places Universe*, where legendary athletes tell stories about their sports.

Jack of All Trades

Bill Simmons did more than write for ESPN. He started his own podcast in 2007. The *BS Report* became a popular staple of ESPN.com and influenced the site to create more podcasts. In 2009 Simmons and coworker Connor Schell created a documentary series called *30 for 30*. They produced 30 films to celebrate the 30th anniversary of ESPN. The series was popular enough to stick around. There have been more than 100 documentaries in the series, and all of them are available on ESPN+. Simmons also created a blog site called Grantland that focused on sports and pop culture. It was popular from 2011 to 2015. And in 2016, he started theRinger.com, which is also a sports and pop culture site.

Chapter Four

GOING PRO

Bill Rasmussen knew before ESPN was launched that the channel needed live sports rights to succeed. That's what led to the deal with the NCAA. ESPN has sustained a partnership with the NCAA since it launched. That partnership grew in 1982, as ESPN started broadcasting college football games. ESPN invested even more into college football in 2012 when it bought the rights to the College Football Playoff (CFP). That proved to be a great deal. The first CFP championship was played on January 12, 2015. The game had over 33 million viewers. That became the most viewed day in

Lee Corso, *left*, and Kirk Herbstreit, *right*, are a big part of *College Gameday*, one of ESPN's most popular shows.

College Gameday

A staple of ESPN college football coverage is its pregame show, *College Gameday*. The show started in 1987. It then began filming live on college campuses in 1993. Former college football coach Lee Corso has been on the show since it started. Each week the show ends with the analysts predicting who will win the featured game of the week. In 1996 Corso started using a prop to show which team he was picking to win. He would put on that team's mascot head and wave to the crowd.

ESPN's history. Since then, every playoff game and every national championship has been broadcast on ESPN.

College sports helped ESPN get off the ground. But professional sports helped it grow quickly. Rasmussen originally wanted ESPN to be a monthly program focused on the New England Whalers. By 1979 the Whalers were in the National Hockey League (NHL) and known as the Hartford Whalers. That made it fitting when the first professional sporting event shown on ESPN was an NHL game between the Whalers and the Washington Capitals in December 1979. ESPN became a regular broadcasting partner for the NHL in the United States. It became the first US network to produce an NHL All-Star Game in 1986. ESPN celebrated its 1,000th NHL broadcast in 1998, so it was surprising when the channel stopped broadcasting the NHL in 2005. ESPN changed that in 2021 by agreeing to a seven-year deal with the NHL. It broadcasts 100 games per season and the Stanley Cup Final.

Superstar quarterback Peyton Manning, *center*, talks to his father Archie, *right*, and ESPN sports broadcaster Mike Tirico during the 1998 NFL Draft.

Sunday to Monday

ESPN aired college football games before it aired any NFL games. But it started a partnership with the NFL in 1980, two years before broadcasting college football. ESPN was the first network to broadcast the NFL Draft live on television. Pete Rozelle, the NFL commissioner at the time, didn't think the draft would draw many viewers. After all, it is just the commissioner reading picks off a card. But the draft has become a popular TV event. Millions of viewers watch the draft on ESPN each year.

Hosts of *ManningCast* Peyton, *left*, and Eli Manning, *right*, were featured as guests during the 2022 Southeastern Conference Championship.

The NFL eventually struck a deal to broadcast games on ESPN in 1987. ESPN has been airing live NFL games every season since. Its coverage got a boost in 1994 when it got the rights to *Sunday Night Football*. Prime-time games at night drew more viewers than afternoon games. That helped grow ESPN's NFL audience.

ESPN switched days in 2006 and started to broadcast *Monday Night Football*, which had aired on ABC since 1970.

Monday Night Football remains a vital part of ESPN's programming. In 2021 ESPN agreed to a new deal with the NFL that granted the network two Super Bowls. In addition, the network added big stars to the broadcast team in 2021. Brothers and former NFL quarterbacks Peyton and Eli Manning did an alternate broadcast on ESPN2 called the *ManningCast*. The Mannings had multiple guests on during the games to make it feel more like a sports conversation show rather than a regular broadcast. *Monday Night Football* got a boost in 2022 when ESPN hired Fox's top broadcasting team of Joe Buck and Hall of Fame quarterback Troy Aikman. An average of 14 million people watch *Monday Night Football* each week.

ESPN added another professional sports league to its schedule in 1990, as it started to broadcast MLB games. That year also saw the start of *Sunday Night Baseball*, MLB's national game of the week. *Sunday Night Baseball* has aired on ESPN every season since it started. It often features the best matchup of the day.

Completing the Cycle

ESPN started broadcasting the NBA in 1982. That deal lasted only until 1984, however. While college basketball thrived on ESPN, the channel didn't carry men's professional basketball for another 18 years. In 2022 the NBA agreed to a deal with ESPN.

That made ESPN the first network to broadcast all four major North American sports leagues.

The network airs NBA regular-season and playoff games, as well as the NBA Draft. ESPN even carries the NBA Summer League, which consists of preseason games featuring players who are trying to make team rosters. ESPN has also been the home of the NBA Finals ever since the 2002–03 season.

Some of the NBA's most iconic moments have happened on ESPN. That includes Game 7 of the 2016 Finals. LeBron James and the Cleveland Cavaliers defeated Stephen Curry and the Golden State Warriors. That game drew an audience of more than 30 million viewers. It is one of the most watched games in NBA history.

In addition to the four major sports, ESPN broadcasts dozens of other American and international leagues. ESPN started broadcasting Major League Soccer when the league started in 1996. When the Women's National Basketball Association (WNBA) began in 1997, ESPN was one of the league's main broadcasting partners. Every season of the WNBA has aired on ESPN, and the network continues to expand its coverage of the league. Years later, ESPN struck a deal with the UFC to have all its fights aired on ESPN's networks as well. That included having all its pay-per-view events streaming on ESPN+.

Holly Rowe, *left*, interviews WNBA star Erica Wheeler after she wins the Most Valuable Player (MVP) Award at the 2019 WNBA All-Star Game.

One of ESPN's biggest international events is the Wimbledon Championships. It is the oldest tennis tournament in the world. ESPN first broadcast the event in 2003 and got exclusive rights to all 14 days of the tournament in 2012. The network's deal with Wimbledon runs until 2035. ESPN also capitalized on Formula One racing's rising popularity in the United States. It broadcast races from 1984 to 1997. Then it started again in 2018. Since then, Formula One has added more races in the United States, and viewership of the sport has gone up.

Chapter Five

FOR THE FANS

In 1993 ESPN broadcast the first Excellence in Sports Performance Yearly Award (ESPY) show. It is now broadcast by ABC. The ESPYs recognize the best male and female athletes of the previous year. They also honor sportscasters, sportswriters, coaches, and other sportspeople.

One award is the Arthur Ashe Award for Courage. It is given to people who "reflect the spirit of Arthur Ashe, possessing strength in the face of adversity, courage in the face of peril and the willingness to stand up for their beliefs no matter what the cost." For the

Arthur Ashe was an American tennis player and influential civil rights activist. He was the first Black man to win singles titles at the US Open, the Australian Open, and Wimbledon.

inaugural ESPYs, Jimmy Valvano was the first recipient of that award. Valvano was the coach of the 1983 NCAA basketball champions, North Carolina State. Besides being a phenomenal coach, he was an inspiration off the court too. Leading up to the award show in 1993, Valvano was diagnosed with bone cancer, which had metastasized, or spread and grown.

Fans used to be the only people voting for the ESPY awards until 2004. However, now the ESPY Select Nominating Committee nominates candidates for the awards, and fans are able to vote online. After all, the company's main goal is simple: "To serve sports fans. Anytime. Anywhere."

Another way ESPN connects fans is through its mobile app. Launched in 2009, the ESPN app started as a way for fans to see scores and highlights from games all around the world. The app let fans select their favorite teams, so those teams' scores would appear at the top of the screen. Fans could also set up

Lost Signal

The success of the ESPN app can be traced back to a massive failure. In 2006 the company launched Mobile ESPN. It was an entire cellular network run by ESPN with a phone designed for sports fans. The phone had a hefty price tag, and there was a monthly service charge for the network. ESPN put $150 million into the project. After poor sales numbers, Mobile ESPN was shut down before the end of 2006. But a lot of the ideas for Mobile ESPN were used on the app a few years later.

In addition to ESPN, *Monday Night Football* can also be viewed on ABC and ESPN+.

alerts on their phones to let them know the final score of a game for any specific team. This kept sports fans in the know even when they couldn't watch live.

Even before the app, there was ESPN360. That was a portion of ESPN's website that aired live games. ESPN360 was eventually put on the app. Fans could not only follow the scores of their favorite teams but also watch the games on their phones. Once ESPN+ was launched in 2018, it became a part of the mobile app. It turned into the main place for fans to watch games on their mobile devices.

Another main way in which ESPN serves sports fans is by providing a platform for fantasy sports. Starting in 2005, consumers could create their own fantasy leagues for free on ESPN. Now more than 20 million people use ESPN.com to run their fantasy leagues.

Let's Make a Deal

Gaining live sporting rights and big sponsorship deals helped ESPN grow. However, some of its most important deals came when ABC bought ESPN from Getty Oil in 1984. The two channels worked separately from each other until 1996. That year, the Walt Disney Company bought ABC and began merging the two stations.

Soon, ESPN employees began broadcasting on ABC. Because it was a cable channel, viewers had to pay extra to get ESPN. Any household that had a TV could access ABC. This helped increase the visibility of ESPN. Sporting events also got more viewers on ABC since people didn't need cable to watch it. Many of ESPN's biggest sporting events still air on ABC to large audiences. This includes *Sunday Night Baseball*, occasional *Monday Night Football* games, the NBA Finals, and more.

Controversies

The relationship between Disney and ESPN has caused backlash. ESPN employs many journalists who cover sports news. A lot of those journalists went to Twitter in November 2019 to promote Disney's new streaming service, Disney+. ESPN reporter Adam Schefter tweeted that Disney+ "will change lives." ESPN received criticism for using journalists as salespeople.

ESPN analyst Steve Young, *left*, talks to Los Angeles Rams quarterback Matthew Stafford after Super Bowl LVI.

Previously, in 2017 some ESPN employees started voicing political opinions on their shows or through social media. A lot of those opinions were criticisms of President Donald Trump. Some viewers, and Trump himself, complained about ESPN's political bias. Viewers claimed they wanted to watch ESPN for sports news, not politics. This led to Pitaro telling employees to avoid politics altogether.

All Sports, All the Time

Going into the 2020s, ESPN had rights to all four major North American professional sports leagues. The network has changed a lot throughout the years. It has expanded to radio shows, podcasts, websites, and streaming services. But at its core, it is a channel dedicated to sports 24 hours a day.

TIMELINE

1978

Bill Rasmussen and Ed Eagan come up with the original idea for ESPN. Rasmussen then purchases land in Bristol, Connecticut, as ESPN's main headquarters.

1979

ESPN airs for the first time starting with *SportsCenter*. It is followed by Game 1 of the American Professional Slowpitch Softball League World Series.

1984

ABC buys ESPN from Getty Oil.

1987

ESPN airs its first NFL game on August 16. Its college football pregame show, *College Gameday,* also has its first broadcast.

1995

ESPN launches its website, ESPN.com.

1996

The Walt Disney Company buys ABC and ESPN.

2002

ESPN agrees to a deal with the NBA to broadcast the league's games.

2015

ESPN has its highest-rated day ever when the first College Football Playoff games are played.

2018

ESPN launches its streaming service, ESPN+.

2021

ESPN agrees to a new deal with the NFL that grants the network two Super Bowls.

IMPORTANT PEOPLE

Chris Berman

One of the original anchors of *SportsCenter*, Chris Berman has worked at ESPN since 1979 and continues to host *NFL Primetime* on ESPN+.

Lee Corso

Lee Corso is a former college football coach who has worked on *College Gameday* since it started in 1987.

Stuart Evey

Evey worked as an executive for Getty Oil. He was the main investor in ESPN and is a big reason it was able to air in 1979.

Tony Kornheiser

Tony Kornheiser was a radio host and writer for the *Washington Post* who became the cohost of *Pardon the Interruption* in 2001. Kornheiser also was an analyst on *Monday Night Football* from 2006 to 2008.

Keith Olbermann

Keith Olbermann anchored *SportsCenter* from 1992 to 1997 alongside Dan Patrick.

Dan Patrick

Dan Patrick was an anchor for *SportsCenter* from 1992 to 1997 alongside Keith Olbermann.

Bill Rasmussen

Bill Rasmussen founded ESPN in Bristol, Connecticut, after purchasing land for satellites to broadcast all over the world. He created the first news channel to show sports 24 hours a day.

Bill Simmons

Boston sports blogger Bill Simmons was hired to write for ESPN.com in 2001. He went on to host the popular podcast the *BS Report* and start the documentary series *30 for 30*.

Stephen A. Smith

Stephen A. Smith started cohosting *First Take* in 2012.

Michael Wilbon

Michael Wilbon, a former *Washington Post* writer, became the cohost of *Pardon the Interruption* in 2001.

GLOSSARY

analyst
In a broadcast, a person who provides details or explanations specific to the topic.

anchor
The person who presents information during a news program.

contract
An agreement between two parties that creates an obligation to perform (or not perform) a particular duty.

documentary
A movie that serves as a factual report on a person or event.

fantasy sports
Games in which participants create virtual teams composed of real players in a given league to compete against each other.

flagship
The most important or largest part of a company.

investor
A person or organization that puts its money into a project, with the expectation of making a profit.

network
A telecommunications system that broadcasts to a wide audience.

prime time
The time when TV audiences are expected to be the largest, typically from 8 to 11 p.m. (EST).

satellite communications
Technology that relays communications via a transponder.

transponder
A device that receives a radio signal and transmits it in a different signal.

MORE INFORMATION

BOOKS

Atli Kjartansson, Kjartan. *Stars of the NBA*. New York: Abbeville Kids, 2021.

Buckley, James, Jr. *Scholastic Year in Sports 2021*. New York: Scholastic, 2020.

Zweig, Eric. *It's a Numbers Game: Football*. Washington, DC: National Geographic Partners, 2022.

ONLINE RESOURCES

To learn more about ESPN, please visit **abdobooklinks.com** or scan this QR code. These links are routinely monitored and updated to provide the most current information available.

INDEX

ABOUT THE AUTHOR

Veteran sportswriter Kristian Dyer currently covers college football for USA TODAY Sports Media Group. He credits his mother, a teacher, with his love for writing. His father would make photocopies at his job of the monthly sports magazine that Kristian wrote while in middle school. He lives in New Jersey with his wife, Sophia, and their adorable four-year-old son, Timothy.